# Spiderwebs to Sky- scrapers

## The Science of Structures

by Dr. David Darling

DILLON PRESS
New York

Maxwell Macmillan Canada
Toronto

Maxwell Macmillan International
New York  Oxford  Singapore  Sydney

## Photographic Acknowledgments

The photographs are reproduced through the courtesy of Unicorn Stock Photos/Doug Adams, Joel Dexter, Robert W. Ginn, Ron P. Jaffe, Martha McBride, D and I MacDonald, MacDonald Photography, Charles E. Schmidt, Dennis Thompson, and Lowell Witcher.

### Library of Congress Cataloging-in-Publication Data
Darling, David J.
    Spiderwebs to skyscrapers : the science of structures / by David Darling.
       p.  cm. — (Experiment!)
    Includes index.
   Summary: Hands-on experiments introduce natural and manmade structures such as a bird's nest and skyscraper and such structural elements as arches, domes, trusses, and beams.
    ISBN 0-87518-478-2
    1. Structural engineering—juvenile literature. [1. Structural engineering—Experiments. 2. Experiments.] I. Title. II. Series: Darling, David J. Experiment!
TA634.D37   1991
624.1'7—dc20
91-4001

Dillon Press
Macmillan Publishing Company
866 Third Avenue
New York, NY 10022

Maxwell Macmillan Canada, Inc.
1200 Eglinton Avenue East
Suite 200
Don Mills, Ontario M3C 3N1

Macmillan Publishing Company is part of the Maxwell Communication Group of Companies.

First edition
Printed in the United States of America
10  9  8  7  6  5  4  3  2  1

# Contents

*What Is Science?* .................................. 4

**1** Preparing the Ground ............................ 9

**2** Shaped for Strength ........................... 15

**3** A Choice of Materials ......................... 23

**4** Sky High ............................................. 32

**5** Buildings for Tomorrow ....................... 40

**6** Home Grown ..................................... 46

*Experiment in Depth* ............................. 53

*Glossary* ........................................... 56

*Index* ............................................... 58

# *What Is Science?*

Imagine gazing to the edge of the universe with the help of a giant telescope, or designing a future car using a computer that can do over a billion calculations a second. Think what it would be like to investigate the strange calls of the humpback whale, dig up the bones of a new type of dinosaur, or drill a hole ten miles into the earth.

As you read this, men and women around the world are doing exactly these things. Others are trying to find out how the human brain works, how to build better rocket engines, and how to develop new energy sources for the twenty-first century. There are researchers working at the South Pole, in the Amazon jungle, under the sea, in space, and in laboratories on every continent. All these people are scientists. But what does that mean? Just what is science?

## Observation

Science is simply a way of looking at the world with an open, inquiring mind. It usually starts with an observation. For example, you might observe that the leaves of some trees turn brown, yellow, or red in fall. That may seem obvious. But to a scientist, it raises all sorts of interesting questions. What substances in a leaf cause the various colors? What happens when the color changes? Does the leaf swap its green-colored chemical for a brown one? Or are the chemicals that cause the fall colors there all the time but remain hidden from view when the green substance is present?

## Hypothesis

At this stage, you might come up with your own explanation for what is going on inside the leaf. This early explanation–a sort of intelligent guess–is called a working hypothesis. To be useful, a hypothesis should lead to predictions that can be tested. For instance, your hypothesis might be that leaves always contain brown, yellow, or red chemicals. It is just that when the green substance is there it masks or covers over the other colors. This is a good scientific hypothesis because a test can be done that could prove it wrong.

## Experiment

As a next step, you might devise an experiment to look more deeply into the problem. A well-designed experiment allows you to isolate the factors you think are important, while controlling or leaving out the rest.

Somehow you have to extract the colored chemicals from a batch of green

leaves and those from a batch of brown leaves. You might do this, for example, by crushing the leaves and putting a drop of "leaf juice" partway up a narrow strip of blotting paper. Hanging the blotting paper so that it dips in a bowl of water would then cause different colored chemicals from the leaf to be carried to different heights up the paper. By comparing the blotting paper records from the green leaves and the brown leaves, you would be able to tell which chemicals were the same and which were different. Then, depending on the results, you could conclude that your first hypothesis seemed right or that it needed to be replaced by a new one.

## Real Science

What we have just described is perhaps the "standard" or "ideal" way to do science. But just as real houses are never spotlessly clean, real science is never quite as neat and tidy as we might wish. Experiments and investigations do not always go the way scientists expect. Being human, scientists cannot control all the parts of an experiment. Sometimes they are surprised by the results, and often important discoveries are made completely by chance.

Breakthroughs in science do not even have to begin with an observation of the outside world. Albert Einstein, for instance, used "thought experiments" as the starting point for his greatest pieces of work—the

special and general theories of relativity. One of his earliest thought experiments was to imagine what it would be like to ride on a light beam. The fact is, scientists use all sorts of different approaches, depending on the problem and the circumstances.

Some important things, however, are common to all science. First, scientists must always be ready to admit mistakes or that their knowledge is incomplete. Scientific ideas are thrown out and replaced if they no longer agree with what is observed. There is no final "truth" in science–only an ongoing quest for better and better explanations of the real world.

Second, all good experiments must be able to be repeated so that other scientists can check the results. It is always possible to make an error, especially in a complicated experiment. So, it is essential that other people, in other places, can perform the same experiment to see if they agree with the findings.

Third, to be effective, science must be shared. In other words, scientists from all over the world must exchange their ideas and results freely through journals and meetings. Not only that, but the general public must be kept informed of what scientists are doing so that they, too, can help to shape the future of scientific research.

To become a better scientist yourself is quite simple. Keep an open mind, ask lots of questions, and most important of all—experiment!

# Preparing the Ground

Structures, large and small, are all around us and serve many different purposes. The ones we tend to think of first are those that people have made, such as houses, bridges, dams, and skyscrapers. Certainly, these can be very spectacular. The Sears Tower in Chicago, for instance, soars 110 stories and 1,454 feet above street level. Twin television masts on the roof take its total height to eighteen hundred feet, or over a third of a mile.

However, there are also many amazing natural structures. Spiders' webs, birds' nests, trees, caves, and mountains are just some of the "buildings" that are put up without any human help. In fact, we could not be builders ourselves if it were not for our skeleton–that vital structure inside each one of us.

### Basics of Building

A structure is simply a thing or a framework that provides support. It might be a bridge that helps hold up a road across a river. Or it might be a house that gives support to the roof and ceiling over our heads.

If the structure is a good one it will be strong enough to stand up to all the forces that are likely to act on it over a long period of time. This requires careful planning and design. Which shapes and arrangements of parts are best suited to the task? What materials should be used?

We also need to think about what a structure will rest upon. How can a building be prevented from simply sinking under its own weight?

◀ *The Sears Tower* (left) *soars above the city of Chicago along the shore of Lake Michigan.*

▲ *Many tall structures such as these skyscrapers rise above the streets of New York City.*

# The Need for Support

## You Will Need:

- A large plastic bowl
- Sand
- Gravel
- Large flat stones
- A square open-topped container
- A ruler
- A pen
- Several heavy books of equal weight
- Four pieces of wood 1/2" thick, 1" long, and 1/2" less wide than the sides of the container (see diagram)
- Four pieces of wood as above but 2" long
- Four pieces of wood as above but 4" long
- A piece of stiff cardboard slightly bigger than the top of the container*

  Note: items marked with a "*" are used only in the "Taking It Further" part of an experiment.

## What to Do:

Pack the flat stones tightly together in the bottom of the bowl to a depth of 2". On top of this put a 2" layer of gravel and, finally, a 2" layer of sand. Make sure that each layer is smooth and even.

On the side of the container mark a scale in tenths of an inch, starting from zero at the open end. Place the open end of the container lightly on the surface of the sand. Its sides represent the outer walls of a building. Gently place one of the books on top of the container. The weight of the book represents the downward load acting on the walls. Look at the scale on the side of the container and write down how much the walls have sunk into the sand. Add several more books, one at a time, and repeat the measurement each time.

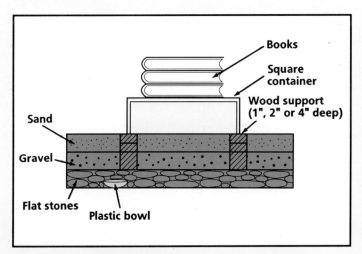

▲ What does this experiment show about the foundations of structures?

continued on next page

Remove the container. Take the four smallest pieces of wood and push them into the sand along the lines made by the sides of the container. The top of the wood should be exactly level with the surface of the sand. Place the container so that its walls sit on the wooden "foundations." Again, gradually load the container with books and after adding each book, measure the amount by which the walls have sunk.

Remove the container and the 1" pieces of wood. Repeat the experiment with the 2" pieces and the 4" pieces. Try to explain what you find. Plot your results in the form of a graph.

### *Taking It Further*:

Place the sheet of cardboard 1" under the surface of the sand. Make sure it is level. Push in the 1" pieces of wood so that they rest on the cardboard. Place the container on the wood and load it with books, one at a time, measuring how much the walls sink as the load is increased. Compare the results with those you obtained earlier for the 1" pieces without the cardboard underneath. What can you deduce from this?

### Firm Foundations

The bigger and heavier a building is, the more it pushes on the ground beneath it. Because of this, all but the lightest structures must sit on specially prepared supports known as foundations.

The soft upper layers of soil are dug away from below where the structure will stand. In the case of an ordinary house, trenches several feet deep are dug along the lines of the supporting walls. Then these trenches are filled with concrete that quickly sets hard.

Larger, heavier structures, such as bridges and skyscrapers, need much deeper foundations to prevent them from sinking. Just how deep the foundations have to be depends on the makeup of the ground beneath the site. Where the ground is soft, the foundation must go down a long way. If there is solid rock near the surface, on the other hand, the foundation can sit directly on it.

▲ *The foundations of the "Georgia Dome" in Atlanta.*

### Skyscraper Cities

Huge skyscrapers such as those in New York City would have been impossible to build in cities such as Houston, Texas, or London, England, until quite recently. The reason is that the island of Manhattan consists almost entirely of bare granite–a very hard and strong type of rock. Houston and London, on the other hand, rest on thick beds of soft clay.

To carry the weight of a building such as a skyscraper, special foundations known as "piles" are used. These are concrete or steel columns hammered into

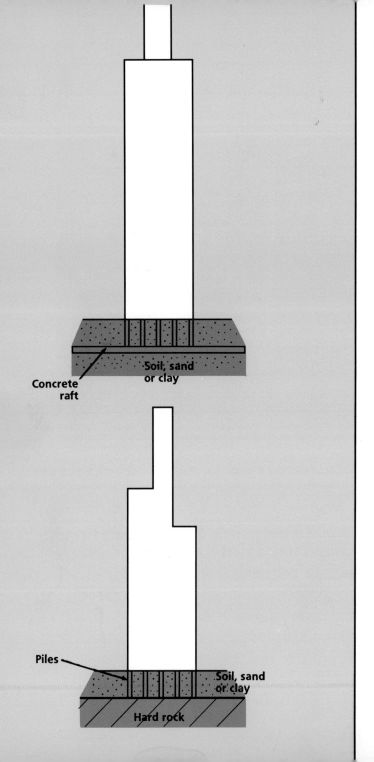

**Concrete raft**

Soil, sand or clay

**Piles**

Soil, sand or clay

**Hard rock**

the ground until they penetrate solid rock or hard-packed soil. Alternatively, piles can be made by boring shafts into the ground and filling them with fresh concrete.

If the underlying rock or firm soil lies too deep to reach with ordinary foundations, engineers may put down a thick raft of concrete right across the site. This spreads the load as widely as possible over the weak soil.

◀ *These drawings show a foundation made with piles driven into rock, and another constructed with a thick raft of concrete.*

# CHAPTER 2

# Shaped
# for Strength

It is much harder to break an egg squeezing it from end to end than by squeezing it across the sides. The reason is not that the eggshell is thicker at the ends, but that it is more highly curved. Some shapes are stronger than others—a fact that is important in the design of every structure, from a sports stadium to a subway.

## Bridge that Gaps

**You Will Need:**

- Four thick, heavy books of equal size
- A piece of stiff cardboard, 10" long and 3" wide
- Several similar coins (pennies or nickels, for example)
- A ruler
- A pencil
- Several other pieces of cardboard, 3" wide and of various lengths*

**What to Do:**

Place two of the books on a table 5" apart. Mark the midpoint of the cardboard. Lay the cardboard across the gap so that the pencil mark is exactly at the middle of the gap. Put down two more books on top of the first pair. Measure the height of the center of the cardboard above the table.

Place a coin on the midpoint of the cardboard. What happens? Measure the height of the midpoint above the table. Put another coin on top of the first and again measure the height of the center of the cardboard. Repeat this until the cardboard bridge collapses.

Draw lines on the cardboard 2" from

*continued on next page*

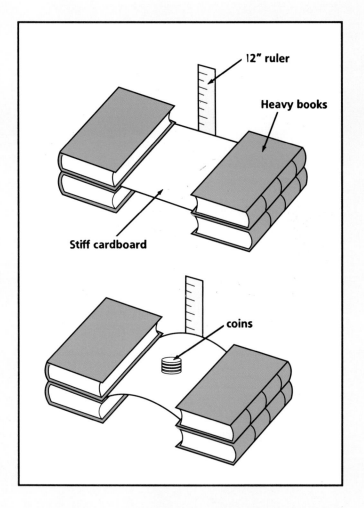

12" ruler

Heavy books

Stiff cardboard

coins

either end, and make folds along these lines. Tuck the 2" flaps under the top pair of books so that the section in between makes a smoothly curving arch. Repeat the experiment above, measuring the height of the top of the arch as you add each coin. What do you notice? Is the cardboard able to support a heavier load when arched or not? Why do you think this should be? Draw a graph for each of your sets of measurements.

***Taking It Further:***
Try doing the experiment with arches of different heights (keeping the gap between the books the same). Which shape of arch is the strongest?

◀*What does this experiment demonstrate about beams and arches?*

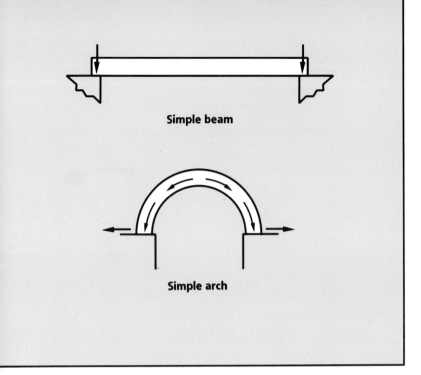

*▲ This drawing shows the forces acting on a beam and an arch.*

## Beams and Arches

Some of the earliest bridges made by people were probably just logs laid between opposite banks of a ditch or stream. The log, used in this way, is an example of a beam–a flat structure supported at each end.

Beams may be made of wood, stone, concrete, iron, or steel. They are very common in all types of buildings, old and

*The famous Gateway Arch rises ▶ near the Mississippi River in St. Louis.*

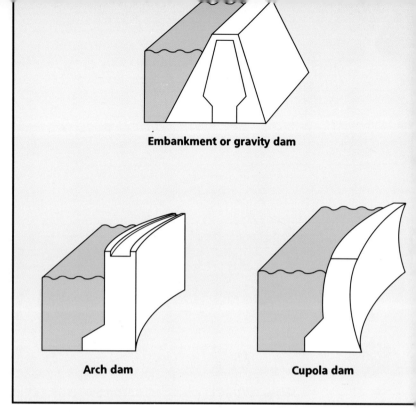

**Embankment or gravity dam**

**Arch dam**

**Cupola dam**

▲ *A gravity dam, an arch dam, and a cupola dam are designed to hold back water in different ways.*

new, because they are so simple to make. But they do have a big drawback. Beams will bend or break if too much weight is put on them. One way to get around this problem is to make the beam quite thick or build it using a very strong material. Alternatively, a different type of structure, such as an arch, may be used in the beam's place.

The shape of an arch gives it great strength. The downward force of any weight is carried away along the arch's smoothly curving sides to its supports. This spreads out the effect of any load. In a beam, by comparison, the load is usually greater at certain points than others, so that the structure has weak spots where it will tend to give way.

## Holding Back the Water

Dams are huge walls of stone or concrete built in the path of a river to form an artificial lake, or reservoir. The reservoir may be used as a water supply for towns and cities, or to produce electricity in a power station at the foot of the dam.

A dam may take one of several basic forms. The simplest is the embankment or gravity dam. This slopes up on each side from a broad base (where it has to withstand the greatest water pressure) to a

▲ *The Grand Coulee Dam in Washington is a huge embankment, or gravity, dam.*

narrow crest. The Grand Coulee Dam in Washington is of this type.  It uses its enormous weight of over twenty million tons to hold back the reservoir behind it.

Less bulky dams, which are cheaper and faster to build, must rely on a stronger shape to resist the force of water acting on them. A dam may be arched, for instance, so that the water pressure is carried outward to the sides. In fact, an arched dam is like a very strong arched bridge lying on its end.

If a dam is arched both up and down *and* from side to side, then it has even greater strength. Such a structure is known as a cupola dam.

## All Trussed Up

A single beam, as we have seen, can easily bend. However, a framework of beams joined together is much stiffer and stronger. The strongest of all frameworks are those in which the beams meet to form triangles. Such an arrangement is called a truss and is based on the principle that a triangle is the hardest shape to twist or bend.

Look in the attic of a house and you will find that the roof is held up by a series

**Believe It or Not!**

THE SAYONO-SHUSENSKAYA DAM IN THE SOVIET UNION WILL BE THE STRONGEST EVER BUILT. IT WILL BE ABLE TO WITHSTAND EIGHTEEN MILLION TONS OF WATER PRESSURE, EQUIVALENT TO OVER THREE MILLION CHARGING ELEPHANTS.

# Testing Frameworks

### You Will Need:

- Stapler and staples
- Strips of cardboard 14" long and 1" wide
- A plastic cup
- Several similar coins (pennies or nickels, for example)
- Tape
- Needle and thread
- Two thick books of the same height

### What to Do:

Cut cardboard strips and use staples to make a square and a triangle as shown. Try pulling the sides of these shapes. What do you notice?

Build a box-shaped framework as shown, using cardboard strips, staples, and tape. Hang the cup by a thread from the center of the framework. Place the two books 12" apart and put the framework evenly between them. Measure the height of the top of the center of the framework. Put a coin in the small box and measure the height again. Do this a number of times and write down your measurements. Can you make the framework collapse completely?

Now make a triangular framework

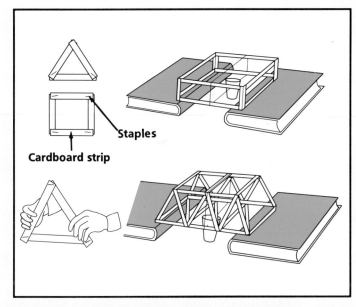

▲ *How do box-shaped and triangular frameworks compare in strength?*

as shown. Repeat the experiment and compare your results. Which framework is stronger? Can you suggest why?

### Taking It Further:

Explore ways of making the box-shaped and triangular frameworks stronger. Try loading them in various ways to find if they have any weak spots.

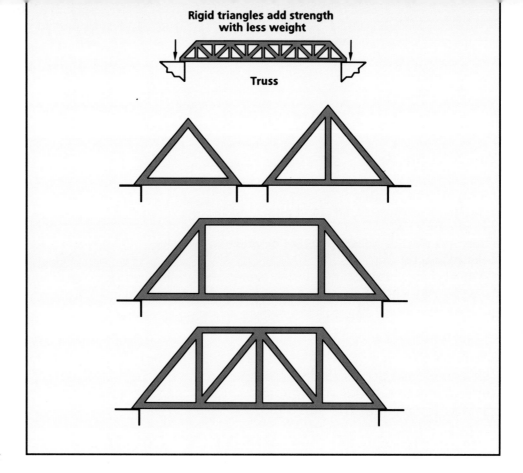

Rigid triangles add strength with less weight

Truss

*This drawing ▶ shows various designs of trusses.*

of trusses made from thick wooden beams. Over the years, engineers have experimented with all sorts of truss designs. For example, wooden trusses were used to support many railway bridges in North America in the last century. Such structures were found to be especially strong if neighboring triangles shared the same side. The common side is known as a king post.

Today, trusses are still used in a wide variety of buildings. They stiffen the supporting structure of tall skyscrapers, form the framework of radio and television masts, and hold up most of the roofs in our houses, stores, offices, and schools.

# CHAPTER 3

# A Choice of Materials

In the past, people built structures using whatever natural materials were available, including animal skins, wood, mud, and stone. But today, in addition to natural materials, we have a wide range of human-made materials. These include bricks, concrete, steel, and even more advanced substances, some of which were developed for use in outer space.

New materials, because of their strength and ability to take on almost any shape, make exciting new types of structures possible. In fact, one of the main tasks of architects now is to select carefully which of the many available materials to use for each part of a new building.

*A steel worker balances on the frame-* ▶
*work of the new building for the Los Angeles County Museum of Natural History.*

# Bricks and Superbricks

**You Will Need:**

- Modeling clay
- Fine straw
- Sand
- Nylon thread
- A 9-ounce plastic cup
- A plastic bowl
- Kitchen scales
- Scissors
- A sharp knife
- A ruler

**What to Do:**

Break off three lumps of clay. Using the ruler and knife, mold and trim the first into a brick 4" long, 3/4" wide, and 1/4" high.

Cut off about 20 pieces of straw, each roughly 1/2" long. Combine these pieces thoroughly with the second lump of clay and make a brick the same size as the first.

Finally, mix about three pinches of sand with the remaining lump of clay before molding it into a third brick. Allow all three bricks to harden overnight.

Poke two small holes in the top of

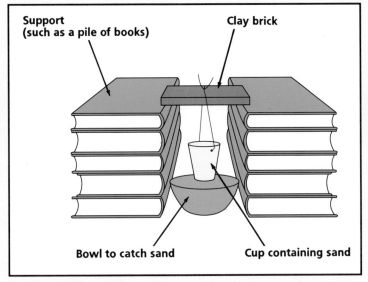

▲ *What does this experiment show about the strength of bricks?*

the cup and pass the nylon thread through. Tie the thread in a loop about 2' long. Pass the thread over the middle of the plain clay brick and rest the ends of the brick on two supports, such as two piles of books, as shown. Place the bowl under the cup.

***Warning:*** Use knives with care. When cutting, make sure your fingers are not in the way.

Begin to slowly pour sand into the cup. Do this until the brick snaps under the load. Pour all the sand back into the cup and weigh it. Make a note of your measurement.

Repeat the experiment with the straw-and-clay brick and with the sand-and-clay brick. What do you notice? Can you explain your results?

***Taking It Further:***
Try using other mixtures of straw and sand. What amount of each produces the strongest brick? What happens if you mix both straw and sand in with the clay? Experiment with other materials in the clay, such as strands of human hair.

You might also try to obtain different types of clay—from river banks or the ground (if there is clay soil in your area) or from craft stores. Which type of clay makes the best bricks?

▲ *A close-up view of bricks arranged in a decorative pattern on a wall.*

## Trials of Strength

In days gone by, the way to see if a new substance or design worked was to build an actual structure, such as a bridge, and hope that it stayed up! Today, however, new building materials are checked thoroughly in laboratories before being used in practice. Equipment is used to measure accurately the strength of a substance under different kinds of stretching, pressing, and twisting forces. Scientists do experiments on the material to find out how it is affected by high and low temperatures, water, and fire.

Often, a pure substance can be made stronger by adding other substances to it. For example, iron becomes tougher and more flexible when turned to steel by mixing it with a small amount of carbon. In a similar way, mud and clay can be made stronger by reinforcing them with sand, straw, animal hair, cow dung, or even blood. The particles of the added substance provide something for the clay particles to bind to and help to stiffen the finished brick.

## The Rock That Pours

Cement is the great, all-purpose building material of today. It consists of a very fine powdered mixture of substances such as calcium silicates and calcium aluminates that are obtained from naturally occurring rocks. When sand and water are added to it, complex chemical reactions take place and the cement sets into a hard, solid mass called concrete.

Aside from being strong, concrete has the big advantage that it can be poured while in the form of wet cement. This makes it ideal for filling in the foundation holes at a building site or for being precast at a factory into any desired shape. The precast sections are then delivered to the building site for assembly.

Like clay, cement can be mixed with various amounts of sand, water, gravel, and other additives to give different types of concrete suitable for different jobs. For large structures, the concrete is given extra strength by molding it around steel bars up to two inches thick. The result is called reinforced concrete.

The steel bars are kept tightly stretched

# Strong, Stronger, Strongest

### You Will Need:

- Cement
- Sand
- Gravel
- Water
- Nylon thread
- A 9-ounce plastic cup
- Strong corrugated cardboard
- A wooden board and old spoon to mix the cement
- Tape
- Scissors
- A ruler

### What to Do:

(Ask a parent or teacher to help you with this experiment.)

Use the cardboard and tape to make a mold. Mix a small quantity of cement, sand, and water in the proportions recommended on the cement container, or ask the adult helper what would be a normal mixture to use. When ready, pour the wet mixture into the first compartment of the mold.

Make a second batch of cement, but this time add some gravel to make a stony mixture. Pour this into the second compartment. Make a third batch, without gravel, but with twice as much sand as before. Pour this into the third compartment.

Allow the mixtures to harden. Test the strength of each brick using the same method as in the experiment "Bricks and Superbricks."

For more on this, see "Experiment in Depth," page 53, section 1.

**Warning:** Cement is harmful if swallowed. Wear old clothes and plastic gloves while doing this experiment. Clean up thoroughly afterward. Never wash unused cement down the sink—it will harden and block the drain.

while the concrete sets, then upon being released they squeeze or "prestress" the concrete, giving it even more strength. Prestressed concrete will not crack even under exceptionally heavy loads.

## Building on Riverbeds

Imagine that you had to build a bridge across a wide river. The design of the bridge calls for tall concrete columns, or piers, to act as supports at regular intervals. How can you put the piers in place without the river washing them away? The answer is by building a temporary dam called a cofferdam where the pier is to go.

Bridge builders sink long beams of hardened concrete, steel, or wood into the riverbed to make a square or circular wall that rises above the water level. Then they

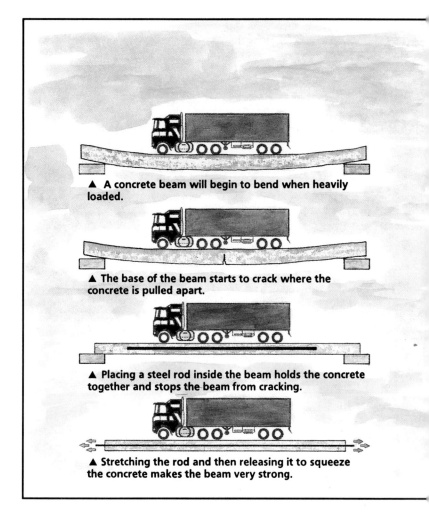

▲ A concrete beam will begin to bend when heavily loaded.

▲ The base of the beam starts to crack where the concrete is pulled apart.

▲ Placing a steel rod inside the beam holds the concrete together and stops the beam from cracking.

▲ Stretching the rod and then releasing it to squeeze the concrete makes the beam very strong.

▲ *Prestressed concrete is used in the construction of many new buildings.*

pump out all the water from inside the cofferdam, so that work can be carried out on the riverbed. The mud and soil is dug away until hard ground is reached, after which cement is poured into the hole to make a sturdy foundation. The pier is built up from the foundation until it rises above the top of the cofferdam. Then the cofferdam is removed and used in building the next pier.

# Make Your Own Cofferdam

### You Will Need:

- **Modeling clay**
- **A plastic cup**
- **Several studded building blocks**
- **Scissors**
- **A drinking straw**
- **A sink**

### What to Do:

Flatten out a lump of the clay so that it is wider than the base of the cup and about 1/2" thick. Stick the clay onto the bottom of the sink. Fill the sink to the depth of the cup. Cut the bottom out of the plastic cup and press this end firmly into the clay. Suck all the water out of the cup with the straw. Push one of the building blocks to the bottom of the clay. Gradually build up a column of blocks until it rises above the rim of the cup. Remove the cup so that the water rushes in around the column.

Compare what you have just done with the description of how a cofferdam works in "Building on Riverbeds."

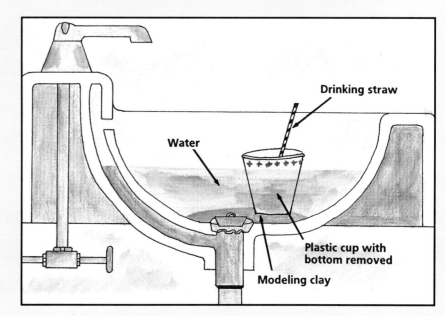

*This drawing shows how ▶ you can build your own cofferdam.*

▲ *The Golden Gate Bridge is supported by thick steel cables.*

### Steeling the Show

Very strong, yet lightweight, steel forms the tough skeleton of many large, modern buildings. Sometimes it is woven into thick cables and used to support suspension bridges such as the Golden Gate Bridge in San Francisco. More often, though, it is made into I- or H-shaped beams, known as girders. These are then joined together to make a framework strong enough to hold the entire weight of a giant building. In fact, it was with the coming of steel frames that a new type of building became possible at the start of this century. That type of building, which is common now in large cities everywhere, is the sky-scraper.

# CHAPTER 4

# Sky High

Tall structures are the best-known and most spectacular human-made landmarks in the world. From the Great Pyramid of Cheops in Egypt to the Empire State Building in New York City, they impress anyone who looks at them.

But tall buildings also serve an important practical purpose today. By spreading upward instead of outward, a skyscraper makes the best possible use of limited space in the center of a city. For example, the 100-story John Hancock Building in Chicago provides homes for fifteen hundred people and work space for a further thirty-five hundred. A restaurant one thousand feet above the ground and a swimming pool and grocery store on the

▲ *The John Hancock Building and other sky-scrapers tower over the city of Chicago.*

forty-fourth floor are among its other sky-high facilities.

### A Pressing Problem

Weight is the biggest problem in the construction of high buildings. The load on the lower sections of a very tall building is only slightly less than that on the foundations. For this reason, the top section of a skyscraper must be made of lighter materials.

Most multistory buildings have frames consisting of steel girders that become thinner toward the top.

As with all structures, a skyscraper must be designed so that the weight of the upper parts is properly supported by the parts underneath. One way to do this is to build a very strong central "core," like the trunk of a tree. The floors of the building are then held up by powerful arching beams, known as cantilevers, that stick out from this core like a tree's branches.

## High Winds beyond This Point

After weight, the next greatest force acting on a tall structure is the pressure of moving air. Winds tend to blow much harder on the upper floors of a skyscraper than on those lower. As a result, there is a powerful bending force on the base.

To resist wind pressure and prevent the top of a building from moving too much, thick steel beams are used to stiffen the outer walls. These may consist of heavy

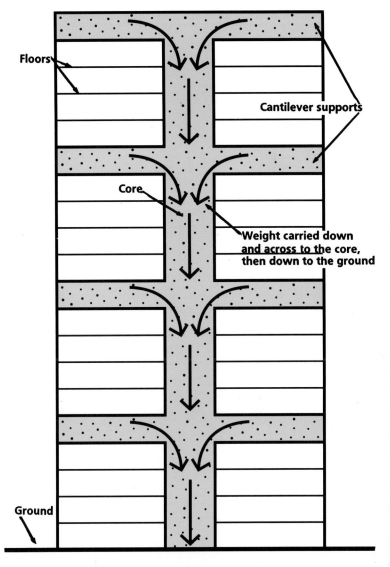

Floors

Cantilever supports

Core

Weight carried down and across to the core, then down to the ground

Ground

▲ *Cantilevers connected to a central core support the great weight of some skyscrapers.*

# Hanging in Midair

### *You Will Need*:

- **Six books about the same size as this one**
- **Several similar coins (pennies or nickels, for example)**
- **A table**

### *What to Do*:

Arrange the books as shown in the diagram. The table represents the core of a skyscraper. The books represent a cantilever, jutting out from the core, supporting the floors of the building. Place several coins at the edge of the top book of the cantilever. These represent the weight of the floors the cantilever has to support. What happens? If the cantilever is not strong enough, reduce the stagger of the books until they can support their load. Notice the type of curve the projecting ends of the books make.

Try arranging the books in a different way so that they stick out as much as the cantilever and support the same load. Is this possible?

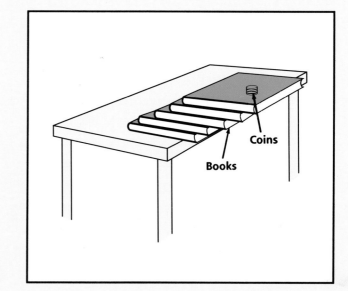

Coins

Books

*What does this experiment demon-* ▶
*strate about the design of cantilevers?*

# Swaying in the Wind

## *You Will Need*:

- **Four sheets of stiff paper, each 2' x 6"**
- **Cardboard strips, as shown in the diagram**
- **Tape**
- **Glue**
- **Scissors**
- **Two rulers**
- **Cutting knife**
- **Pen**
- **A toothpick**
- **Blow dryer**
- **A table or kitchen counter next to a tiled wall**

## *What to Do*:

Make a model skyscraper as shown in the diagram. Cut four strips of cardboard each 25" long and 2" wide. Draw a line down the middle of each strip, then score and bend the cardboard along this line. Make a cut 1" long from one end of the line and fold out the two flaps. Glue the sheets of paper to the strips of cardboard to make the structure as shown. Tape the cardboard flaps securely to the table so that one side of the model is almost up against the wall. Tape the toothpick into the right-hand corner of the cardboard

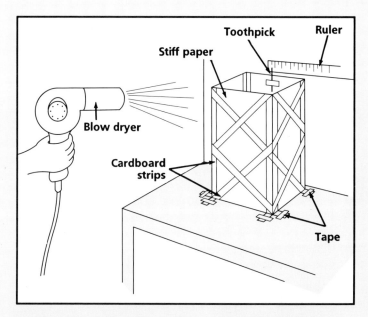

▲ *This drawing shows how to test the design of your model skyscraper in a "wind."*

frame that is against the wall so that it sticks up at least 1" from the top of the model. Tape one of the rulers to the wall so that the toothpick is pointing at the zero end of the scale. Hold the blow dryer 1' from the top of the left-hand

*continued on next page*

wall and turn it on to the coolest, highest speed setting. Notice what happens to the model skyscraper. Record how far the toothpick has moved from its zero setting. This gives a measure of the sway of your structure.

Now try adding the X-shaped cardboard supports. Glue these securely to each side of the model. Position the blow dryer as before, turn it to the same setting, and measure the amount of sway. What do you conclude?

***Taking It Further*:**
Experiment with your own methods to reduce the sway in your model skyscraper. For example, try adding extra strips of cardboard to stiffen the structure or devise ways to make the lower sections of the model heavier than the top. You might also look at how the shape of a structure affects the amount it sways. For example, try testing a structure that tapers toward the top.

For more on this, see "Experiment in Depth," pages 53-54, section 2.

beams that run right across and around the skyscraper or diagonal beams that make an X-shaped pattern. Diagonal beams were originally used to stiffen just the central core of tall buildings, but now they are also found on the outside walls.

Another way to reduce sway is to make a skyscraper narrower at the top than at the bottom. This lessens the area of the walls where the wind speeds are highest, so that the sideways force on the top parts of the building is lowered.

Even the strongest skyscrapers, however, sway to some extent. The wind force acting over one face of a tall building may be as much as two thousand tons. This can cause the top of a building such as the World Trade Center in New York, which is 110 stories high, to sway back and forth by as much as 36 inches.

## Safety Checks
The design of a new skyscraper has to be

▲ *Tall skyscrapers such as the twin towers of the World Trade Center in New York City may sway as much as 36 inches in a strong wind.*

thoroughly tested to make sure that it can stand up to all the forces that will act on it. To determine the effect of winds, for example, a plastic scale model may be built that has small tubes with openings at various heights. This model is then put in front of a set of powerful fans. As the moving air from the fans strikes the model, the amount by which the air pressure in the tubes is increased can be measured. If the bending force of the wind seems too high then the design may have to be altered, perhaps by adding more steel beams. Sometimes a model will be made of the entire downtown area of a city. This is because the winds acting on a new building will be determined partly by the position and size of other skyscrapers nearby.

Much use is also made of computers in the early stages of skyscraper design. Programs running on a computer help to show how important parts of the design are affected by the loads they have to bear. The computer can produce color pictures highlighting regions where the force is most intense.

In some parts of the world, earthquakes are a threat–especially to tall buildings that might easily topple over. Skyscrapers in places such as San Francisco need to have special foundations that can absorb the shock of earthquakes. They also need to have supporting frameworks that can bend and vibrate without giving way. Special equipment known as a "shaking table" allows engineers to test whether a new design would be safe in an earthquake.

# A Model City

### *You Will Need:*

- **Containers of various sizes and shapes, including boxes and plastic bottles**
- **A large wood or cardboard base**
- **A blow dryer**
- **A desk lamp or flashlight**
- **Pins**
- **Paper**
- **Scissors**
- **Tape and glue**

### *What to Do:*

Stick the containers to the base to make a model of a city. Make the model realistic by drawing out a street plan and arranging the buildings in well laid out blocks.

Cut small strips of paper and fold them around the pins to make little flags. The paper should be able to spin around freely if you blow on it. Stick the flags on various parts of your model—at street level and on the tops and sides of buildings.

Set up the fan so that it is level and pointing at the tops of your model skyscrapers. Turn all the flags so that they are at right angles to the direction the fan is pointing. Turn on the fan. What happens to the flags? Which parts of the city have felt the greatest effect of the wind? Move the fan to a new position, set up the flags as before, and repeat the experiment. Describe your results.

Darken the room and use the lamp or flashlight to represent the sun. Move the light over the model in a high arc. Notice how the shadows of the buildings move and change size. Do any of the shadows of the taller buildings extend beyond the downtown area? If so, these shadows might fall on parts of the city where many people have their homes. Decide if this is a problem and, if so, redesign your model to reduce the effects of shadowing.

### Taking It Further:

Invent your own section of a city or use ideas from a city that you know well.

You might also study the effects, for example, of demolishing one of the skyscrapers in your model and replacing it by a much higher one.

For more on this, see "Experiment in Depth," page 54, section 3.

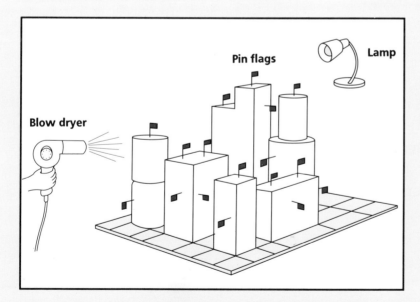

Pin flags    Lamp

Blow dryer

◄ *How does the design of your model city affect the wind currents and shadows?*

# CHAPTER 5

# Buildings for Tomorrow

How will humans be living fifty years from now? Five miles up in soaring skyscraper cities? Or perhaps in homes underground? One thing seems certain: the buildings and communities in which people spend much of their lives will be very different in years to come than they are today.

Our current supplies of fuels are gradually running out, while at the same time the earth's population is rising steeply. This will mean that buildings in the next century will have to be much more energy efficient. They will need to be easier and cheaper to build, and able to use energy sources, such as heat from the sun, which will not run out.

## EXPERIMENT!

### Super Structures

***You Will Need:***

- **Modeling clay**
- **Swizzle sticks**

***What to Do:***
Break off small pieces of clay, roll them into balls, and use these to hold together the swizzle sticks in various arrangements. Try building a dome-shaped structure such as the one shown here from a series of interlocking triangles. Test this structure by pressing down on it. Is it strong? If so, can you explain why?

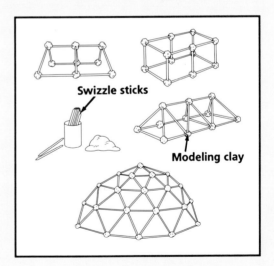

Swizzle sticks

Modeling clay

## Geodesic Domes

Not all buildings in which people live, work, or play need to have supporting walls inside. A dome-shaped structure will support itself because of the way the weight of the building is gradually directed down the curving sides of the building to the ground. However, a round dome is difficult to make. Much easier to assemble is a dome, known as a geodesic dome, constructed from flat triangular panels which fit perfectly together.

"Geodesic" comes from two Greek words meaning "earth dividing." In the geodesic dome, a half-sphere is divided into a number of interlocking triangles—the more triangles used, the stronger the structure. All the sides of these triangles, usually made of steel, work together to carry the load evenly.

Geodesic domes are simple to build, strong and lightweight, and can be used for everything from tents to sports stadiums. Because they have no internal walls, the domes allow air to circulate freely around, making them easy to keep at a steady, comfortable temperature throughout.

The famous American architect Buckminster Fuller even suggested that entire cities might someday be enclosed within giant geodesic domes. Since no beams are needed to support them, such domes could be almost any size. Protected by a clear bubble of plastic, the city's inhabitants would never have to suffer from bad weather. On hot summer days, the dome's panels could be darkened to shield the city from the sun's glare. Such domes might be especially useful to protect future human colonies on other planets or the moon.

# Earth Shelters

### You Will Need:

- **Two shoe boxes**
- **Two maximum and minimum thermometers (ask your teacher or parent if you are not sure where to obtain them). A maximum and minimum thermometer records the highest and lowest temperatures during a given period. Its indicators can be reset using a small magnet.**

### What to Do:

Do this experiment in summer when it is warm outside and the ground is dry.

Reset the thermometers using the magnet and place one thermometer in each of the shoe boxes. Early in the morning, put one of the boxes in a hole in the ground and cover it with about 6" of earth. Put the other box on top of the ground a few feet away from the buried box. The next morning, open both boxes and make a note of the highest and lowest temperatures recorded by the thermometers. What are your results? Can you explain them?

### Taking It Further:

Repeat the experiment at different times of the year. Try placing the bur-ied box at a variety of depths. Does this affect the range of temperatures you record? Are the results different if you bury them in sand instead of soil?

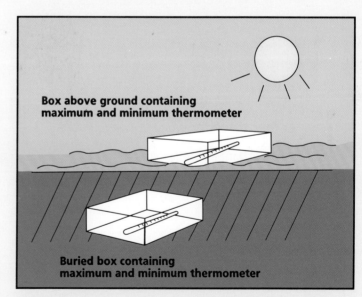

Box above ground containing maximum and minimum thermometer

Buried box containing maximum and minimum thermometer

▲ *Which thermometer records the highest and lowest temperatures?*

◀ *The Geosphere at Epcot Center in Florida is an example of a geodesic dome.*

### Building Underground

Underground or "earth-sheltered" buildings are becoming increasingly popular. They take advantage of the fact that soil does not let heat pass through it very easily. In fact, nine feet below the surface, the temperature stays between 50°F and 68°F whatever the weather. Since very little heat can pass through its walls, an underground home is easy to keep warm in winter and remains comfortably cool even on the hottest summer day.

Often, the shell of an underground structure is made from precast sections of reinforced concrete. These are strong enough to withstand the weight of a large amount of overlying earth and the sideways pressure of soil on the walls.

# Design a Home

***You Will Need:***

- **Pencil, paper, and ruler**
- **A variety of building materials**

***What to Do:***

Your goal is to design and build a model of a house of the future. Decide on the type of home. Where will it be built—in a city, in the country, on a mountainside, in a desert, by the seashore? How many people will it accommodate? How will it be heated or cooled?

Sketch plans of the rooms. Is there easy access from one room to the next? Are the rooms a good size and shape for their purpose? How will the building be supported? What materials will you use?

Decide on the position of doors, windows, stairs, and other important features. Will your house be easy to keep at a comfortable temperature in both the winter and summer? Will it have enough natural light during the day?

When you have made detailed plans and sketches, try to make a model of the house using materials such as cardboard, balsa wood, and plastic.

### Taking It Further:
You might get ideas for your model by looking in magazines about houses or books on energy-efficient homes. Look more closely at the houses in your neighborhood. Try to combine the best features, plus some of your own, in your design.

For more about this, see "Experiment in Depth," pages 54-55, section 4.

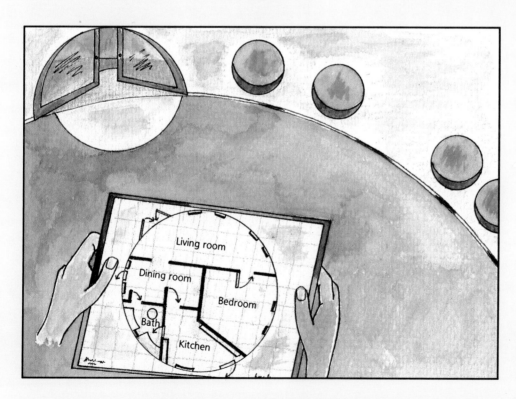

Living room

Dining room

Bedroom

Bath

Kitchen

◄ *What are the features of your model house of the future?*

# CHAPTER 6

# Home Grown

Many of the world's most amazing structures are not made by human beings at all. Termites, for example, build tall towers of mud and saliva, a mixture that sets as hard as concrete. Rising up to twenty feet high, these towers provide ventilation for the main nest, which is below ground level.

Spiders build webs from a silky substance that is stronger than steel if stretched out to the same thickness. In fact, at an army research center near Boston, scientists are trying to develop superstrong, lightweight fibers based on spiders' silk. These could be used, for example, in parachutes or bullet-proof clothing. We can learn much from the structures and building materials of animals and plants.

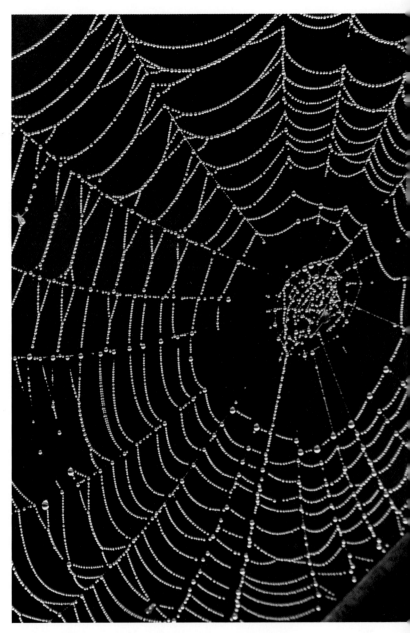

▲ *A spiderweb is constructed of extremely lightweight but strong fibers.*

# Webs: A Fly's-Eye View

**You Will Need:**

- A magnifying glass
- A microscope and clean slide
- A spider's web

**What to Do:**
Find a spider's web and examine it carefully with the magnifying glass. Sketch or describe any features you can see on the strands. If possible, identify the type of spider that made the web.

Place the slide behind a section of the web and lift it away so that one or two strands stick to the middle of the glass. Put the slide under the lowest power of the microscope. Make a careful sketch of what you see. Do some strands of the web appear different from others? Increase the magnification and see if this brings any more detail into view.

Repeat these observations with webs made by other kinds of spiders.

## Spider Traps

The webs of spiders work in two main ways. Some webs have "capture" threads that are covered with small sticky droplets to ensnare prey. Other webs, built by a different family of spiders, are dry. These dry webs consist of a fuzz of fine threads with loops and barbs for holding on to their victims.

## The Master Builder

The largest and most spectacular animal constructions are the dams and lodges built by beavers in North America. The beaver's long front teeth grow throughout its life and are kept to a manageable length by gnawing at the trunks and branches of trees. A beaver can fell a tree three feet thick. It floats the wood down the river to the site where the dam is to be built. The animal carries mud and stones in its forepaws and adds them to the branches to form the dam wall.

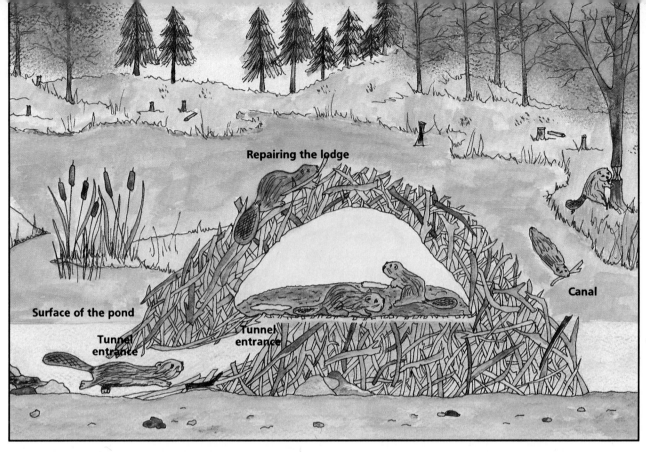

**Repairing the lodge**

**Canal**

**Surface of the pond**

**Tunnel entrance**

**Tunnel entrance**

▲ *This is an artist's cutaway picture of the activity in and around a beaver lodge.*

Some distance behind the dam, in the lake that has been formed, the beavers build a dome-shaped "lodge." This provides a warm, safe shelter for one or more family groups. The entrances are underwater so that they remain open even when the surface is frozen over in winter.

Beavers can strip the lake shore of all trees to a distance of several hundred yards. When they have done this, they simply move on to a new site. Eventually, the old site becomes clogged with mud. New vegetation then grows on the rich soil created by the beavers' building.

◄ *A beaver dam.*

# Make like a Bird

### You Will Need:

- An abandoned bird's nest
- Rubber gloves
- Several sheets of paper
- Measuring scales
- Various materials for building your own nest, such as twigs, feathers, and mud

### What to Do:

Make sure that the bird's nest is no longer in use before you touch or remove it. Use rubber gloves if you wish, since the nest is likely to contain various bugs. Weigh the whole nest. Observe closely how it has been made.

◀ *A robin's nest with eggs.*

How does it hold itself together? How have the various materials been used in its construction? Carefully pull the nest apart over a sheet of paper and sort the contents into piles—twigs on one sheet of paper, feathers on another, and so on. Weigh the various piles and work out what percentage each represents of the total weight of the nest.

Now attempt to make your own nest from scratch. Can you equal or improve on the bird's design? Remember, only use building materials that would be available to the bird, though these could include human-made articles that have been thrown out.

**Believe It or Not!**

HOME SWEET HOME

A NEST BUILT BY A PAIR OF BALD EAGLES NEAR ST. PETERSBURG, FLORIDA, WAS NEARLY NINE FEET ACROSS AND OVER EIGHTEEN FEET DEEP. IT WEIGHED SEVERAL TONS.

**This section looks at some of the experiments described in this book in more detail.**

**1. Strong, Stronger, Strongest, page 27.** Cement is an excellent material for testing the strength of some of the shapes mentioned in this book since it can be cast into any form. For example, molds could be made of beams and various types of arches. When hard, the structure could then be loaded either by putting weights on top or hanging them below. This kind of loading stretches the material by creating tension. More advanced students might also try subjecting concrete beams, arches, and other shapes to a force of compression. Loading a beam with heavy weights along its length or squeezing the beam lengthwise in a vise are alternate ways of doing this. Safety goggles should be worn for such an investigation because of the risk of flying fragments when the concrete breaks.

**2. Swaying in the Wind, pages 35-36.** It is important in this experiment that the attachment of the model skyscraper to the table, or other surface, be very secure. Otherwise, the measurement will include some "give" of the base as well as bending of the whole structure. If the tape does not prevent the bottom of the structure from lifting away in the airstream then the experiment is not a fair one. This is because it would be allowing an uncontrolled factor to interfere with the quantity under investigation–namely, the bending of the model skyscraper in the artificial wind.

As with all the experiments in this book, the method given is only a suggestion. You should try out your own ideas and modifications. Perhaps you can devise a better way of building the skyscraper or measuring the amount of swaying.

Try making models of famous skyscrapers such as the Sears Tower or John Hancock Center in Chicago, or the Empire State Building or World Trade Center in New York. Remember, however, that this will not give a fair comparison of the amount of sway in these buildings since you will not have taken into account differences in internal structure, weight distribution, and so on.

### 3. A Model City, pages 38-39.

Instead of an entire section of a city , you could focus on just a small cluster of skyscrapers. One of the effects of tall buildings is that they tend to cause winds to spiral down to street level. You could study this by putting several high structures together, marking their sides and the model streets with pin flags, and then directing air from a powerful fan at the tops of the buildings. Can you produce a spiraling air pattern? If so, can you get rid of the wind at street level by rearranging the buildings or spacing them farther apart? Read about this effect and find out how architects attempt to avoid the problem in practice.

### 4. Design a Home, pages 44-45.

This project would be suitable for, say, a science fair or a school competition. It could be used to bring together ideas discussed in a course on structures, reconservation. Working alone or in groups, entrants could display their results in the form of plans, artwork, and models, and be available to answer questions about their designs.

As well as homes, the project might involve, for example, plans for a new library, school, sports center, or shopping mall. A local architect might be invited to act as judge and prizes could be given to the winners in various age categories.

**arch**—a curved structure resting on upright supports that is used for bearing a load

**beam**—a straight, flat piece of material supported at either end

**cantilever**—an arm that sticks out from a central support and that can be used to bear a load

**cement**— a gray, powdery substance made up of certain kinds of ground-up rocks. When mixed with sand and water, it hardens to form concrete.

**cofferdam**—a water-tight enclosure, from which the water can be pumped, to give a dry foundation for bridges and piers

**concrete**—a hardened mixture of cement, sand, and water which may also include small stones and steel rods for extra strength

**cupola dam**—a dam that curves both from side to side and from top to bottom

**earth-sheltered building**—a building that is partly or completely covered by soil

**foundation**—a hard base, below ground level, upon which a building rests

**geodesic dome**—a dome-shaped structure built from flat, interlocking panels of identical shape

**girder**—a long beam, usually made of iron or steel, used for structural support

**gravity dam**—a dam that is much wider at the bottom than at the top. It relies on its own weight, rather than a curved shape, to hold back the water.

**piles**—columns of steel and concrete that are driven deep into the ground to provide a firm foundation for buildings such as skyscrapers

**prestressed concrete**—concrete containing steel rods that are held tightly stretched while the concrete is setting. This is the strongest type of concrete.

**reinforced concrete**—concrete that has been strengthened inside with steel rods

**shaking table**—a piece of equipment used by scientists to study how earthquakes might affect a new building. It consists of a platform that can be loaded and vibrated in various ways.

**steel**—a metal made by mixing molten iron with a small amount of carbon. This makes it stronger than iron alone.

**suspension bridge**—a bridge whose weight is supported by steel cables slung over the top of tall metal piers

**truss**—a framework of wood or iron, usually in the form of interlocking triangles, that provides support

# INDEX

arch, 18

beam, 17-18, 31, 33-36

cantilevers, 33
cement, 28, 29
cofferdam, 28-29
concrete, 28

dams, 18-20

earthquakes, 38
"earth-sheltered" buildings, 44
Einstein, Albert, 6-7

foundations, 12-14
Fuller, Buckminster, 41

geodesic domes, 41
girders, 31
Golden Gate Bridge, 31

Grand Coulee Dam, 20

Houston, Texas, 13

John Hancock Building, 32

London, England, 13

Manhattan, island of, 13

piles, 13-14

San Francisco, 38
science: experiments in, 5-6; hypotheses in, 5; observations in, 4-5; truth in, 7

Sears Tower, 9
spiderwebs, 46-47

termite towers, 46
truss, 20-22

World Trade Center, 36

## About the Author

Dr. David Darling is the author of many science books for young readers, including the Dillon Press Discovering Our Universe, World of Computers, and Could You Ever? series. Dr. Darling, who holds degrees in physics and astronomy, has also written many articles for *Astronomy* and *Odyssey* magazines. His first science book for adult readers, *Deep Time* (1989), has been described by Arthur C. Clarke as "brilliant." He currently lives with his family in England, where he writes and lectures to students in schools.